One Day with Two Leaders

One Great, One Terrible

Even a Bad Leader Can Be a Great Example

D. Lane Stephens

ISBN-13: 978-0-9832082-1-1

DEDICATION

This book is dedicated first and foremost to my wife, Michele, who has helped me be a better person. She is always there for me being incredibly supportive. She will always tell me what I need to hear and not just what I want to hear. She has been there for me and for all of her family and friends with no questions asked.

It is also dedicated to all of those leaders that I have worked with...some good, some not so good, and some so horrible at leading that they had absolutely no reason ever being given a leadership position. However, as you will see in this book, even a bad leader can serve as a great example.

INTRODUCTION

This book will take you through a typical day of a leader of an organization comparing the styles and behaviors of two leaders...one great leader and one absolutely horrible leader. One can see the two differences in the leaders and be able to ask themselves how do I operate today and how should I be operating? It may only serve as a reminder for some of you but as we all know sometimes things go so well we stop doing them.

I was inspired to write this book by the experiences I had working with the offices that reported to me through the years. When I would visit those offices as the Vice-President of Sales for a geographic sales region, I could sense a great leader by walking into the office and spending time with the people. Great performing offices of great leaders had "it". "It" was hard to define but you could tell an office that had "it" and those that did not.

The offices that had great leadership had people who were smiling, they were energetic, they were excited and they could not wait to tell you what they were accomplishing. They knew where the organization was headed, what the plan was to get there, and how they were going to celebrate when they got there. They took responsibility for their results and they did not spend their time whining or beating a dead horse about what they did not have. They looked for ways to win and win the right way.

They had "it" and the "it" was provided by the atmosphere the leader created in an office. The leader did it with a clear vision, great communication skills, and an energy that just pulled you to that leader like a magnet.

Those leaders also knew it was what they did everyday that counted. Leadership is not a spectator sport. It is showing up everyday and what they did everyday made the difference. Being a leader isn't something you do on Thursdays. You do it every day.

I hope your organization has "it"!

I also want to thank every one of the managers and leaders I had the opportunity to work with through the years. I learned something from everyone of you!

One Day With Two Leaders

CHAPTER 1

Lenny the Leader walked into the office that morning with a smile on his face. He stopped and spoke to everyone he saw on the way in the door, asking how they were doing and how their families were doing. He had a spring in his step and people could see how enthusiastic and energetic he was.

They could also see that he didn't just go through the motions when he talked with folks. He stopped, he looked them in the eye, and he listened. He didn't answer a cell phone, he didn't send emails on his BlackBerry and he did not look past the person. He was there. He was in that moment. At that particular moment, his associates (called employees in many organizations) felt that they were special. Lenny the Leader cared.

He spoke to everyone along the way. He didn't just speak to the executives or his direct reports. He treated everyone the same way. It did not matter whether it was the janitor, the head of sales, the admin, or the delivery person. He spoke to everyone and everyone he came into contact with felt rejuvenated. They knew he cared for them, and they knew they liked being with him.

His contagious enthusiasm and energy remained with all of the people he had spoken to that morning. Those folks passed it along to everyone they saw that day. They spoke to everyone. They asked how they were doing and they cared for their associates. They looked for ways to help everyone do a better job. The enthusiasm and energy flowed through the organization!

The people Lenny spoke to looked for ways to do a better job. They looked for ways to help the company make money. This was not a job. This was a mission. They were ready to succeed. They thought what a great place to work!

Down the road at a different company, Mike the Boss walked into the office, staring straight ahead, talking on a cell phone, and never looked at any of his employees. He never spoke to an employee as he stormed back to his office. He had a scowl on his face as he went into his office and closed the door.

The employees who saw Mike the Boss come in all wondered to themselves, what did I do? I must be in trouble. The Boss didn't speak to me. I thought I was doing Ok, but maybe I am not.

The people who saw Mike the Boss come in also wondered if the company was in trouble. Mike the Boss looked awfully angry and he was on that cell phone and he shut himself in the office. They wondered what was wrong with the company. They each silently asked themselves, I wonder if the business is going under. I wonder if I am going to be fired.

The employees were suddenly suspicious of the other employees. Maybe they will keep their jobs and I will be fired. Did one of them say something ugly about me to Mike the Boss? I will not help that person. I need to look better than them just in case we are downsizing. If I help them, it may hurt my chances of keeping my job.

The employees also thought about how hard they worked and that they could not wait until the weekend. They watched the clock tick toward quitting time.

CHAPTER 2

Lenny the Leader continued to his office to meet with his managing associates. They were all gathering in the conference room for their weekly meeting with Lenny. Lenny spoke to all of them just as he had all of the other associates. He had the same enthusiasm, the same energy and the same caring as he did earlier.

Lenny's people communicated to him what was going on in sales. They communicated to him about what was going on in operations. They communicated what was going on with the profit numbers. They also communicated what challenges they were facing.

They told Lenny both good news and bad news. They did not couch anything. They told it like it was without fear of being admonished for bringing bad news.

They put everything in the context of the long term goals of the company. They knew where the company was going and they knew what the goal was. Lenny had created the vision with the help of his associates, and they were all marching to the same music. They were in sync. They were not working against each other.

Each of the managing associates could tell you in very few words what the company mission was and they could tell you what made their company the best in the business through the eyes of the customer. They could tell you exactly where they stood toward achieving that mission. More importantly, so could all of the other associates.

They all knew where the company was going, how they were going to get there, and what they were going to do when they achieved the short term goal. They knew because Lenny made sure that the vision was clear, concise and compelling and because communication was valued in the organization. Lenny knew that if everyone knew where they were headed, the associates would take them there.

The associates could make decisions in the context of the mission. They were empowered because they knew where they were headed and that they could make decisions that would help the organization achieve that destination.

The associates also knew that they could make decisions without worrying about being second-guessed. They knew they were trusted as well as valued and that mistakes were learning opportunities. They did not fear the consequences of a bad decision. Even without negative consequences, decisions made were usually very good because they were all well trained, well informed, and their decisions were made based on facts, data and logic.

When the managing associates brought up challenges, they didn't just bring up the problems and ask Lenny to fix the issue. They told him the challenge and they also brought solutions they felt could solve the challenge.

They also discussed everything as a group and all participated. This was an organization that recognized that a decision in one area impacts another area and that they needed to make sure the company was in alignment.

The associates also knew that if they accomplished the mission that they would be rewarded. Their compensation plans were aligned with the results the company needed to attain. If they were hitting their targets and making money in their compensation plans, the company was making money. At the same time, if the company was making money they were making money. Everyone's compensation aligned at all levels of the company.

The meeting today was over in 23 minutes. Lenny had prepared an agenda prior to the meeting and the expectation of the Managing Associates was that they would be prepared prior to the meeting. Their meetings did not automatically go an hour. If they were through with the important items, they were done with the meeting.

Minutes of the meeting were circulated quickly after the meeting. The managing associates could then review important items with the other associates. Everyone knew what was happening and why. They also could translate any action items to what they needed to do in their roles.

Down the road, Mike the Boss, held his weekly meeting as well. The Employee Managers gathered and made sure they were in the room on time because Mike the Boss would get really angry if you were late, even if you were late because you were dealing with a customer. The expectation was that you made the meeting no matter what and you had better be on time or you would face the wrath of Mike the Boss.

Mike the Boss came into the meeting late. He was late because he had not been prepared for the meeting and he needed to look at some numbers. The employees knew there was a double standard. One needed to do as Mike said and not what he did.

The Manager Employees communicated mostly good news and very few challenges as they did not want to get "shot" as the messenger. Mike the Boss had a tendency to do that. If an employee brought him bad news, he would question the news, question the messenger of the bad news, and ultimately ridicule the bearer of the bad news. The point would be debated and so discussed that ultimately they would all decide the challenge was not all that bad and did not stand in the way of them getting the mission accomplished.

The other employees knew nothing about the meeting topics and what may have been decided as the managing employees felt that information was power and the managing employees felt they needed to keep the information to themselves. That was their power.

The employees could not make decisions because they did not know where the company was headed and if they did make a decision they would be in trouble if it did not work out. If their decision did not work out, they would be blamed and they would lose their job. As a result, they took the safe route and did not make any decisions. They bumped everything up to their Employee Manager.

They also knew that if they made a good decision, they would never get credit for it as the Employee Manager would take credit for the decision. They knew they would never know if that happened as Mike the Boss never talked with them or even to them so they had no chance to get recognized.

The Employee Managers also very rarely made decisions and bumped most stuff to Mike the Boss. Mike the Boss wanted to make all of the decisions but also whined about the employees not being able to make decisions and how he had to do everything in the organization.

Decision making was slow because all had to be run through Mike the Boss. Delays would occur because the employees were afraid to go to Mike the Boss. The employees procrastinated and then even when they did go to Mike more delays occurred because Mike had so many decisions on his plate. He was not going to delegate that decision making power.

CHAPTER 3

Next up on Lenny the Leader's calendar was an interview with a top candidate for an open sales position. The position was open because the previous sales rep had been promoted to Sales Manager. The previous Sales Manager had been promoted to National Sales Manager reporting directly to Lenny.

Lenny and his organization always tried to promote from within the organization. It always sent the right message to the other employees and helped them retain top talent.

Lenny also knew that too often you have no idea what you are really getting from outside the organization when you hire externally. He had too many previous experiences where the external hires did not live up to their press clippings. Their resumes looked great on paper, the qualifications were there, and the references always spoke highly of the candidate. He knew that no one was going to put a bad reference down on the resume. All of the references would do nothing but heap praise on Lenny about the candidate.

What he found was that too often he would be stuck with someone with Permanent Potential. They always had the potential to be great but for some reason did not have the internal fire to actually fully achieve that potential. They had Permanent Potential.

Lenny also knew that this new Sales Manager was going to be great at the role. He knew one had to be careful about promoting some sales reps as not every great sales rep can make a great sales manager. Many times you not only lose a great sales rep but you get a poor manager when you just promote someone because the sales results were there. You take a double hit with a bad promotion.

Lenny knew that would not be the case as the rep who had been promoted had been in the Succession Management Program for the past year and had actually been performing some management duties while still performing her rep duties. She had grown to the point where she could receive her satisfaction from watching her people succeed. She was mature enough to not allow her ego and drive for recognition that most successful reps have as reps to interfere with her being a manager. She wanted to succeed as a Manager for the right reasons.

Lenny had been careful to make sure that his organization did not require someone to be promoted to Manager to feel valued by the organization. He knew that some companies make tragic mistakes when they have an organization where you indeed have to go into management to feel valued.

Lenny also knew that this was probably a very good candidate. He knew that this candidate, like all candidates applying for a position with the company, had gone through a thorough screening by his organization.

In his company's process, candidates interviewed with several people within the organization. The hiring manager would have the initial interview to explain the position, describe the company, and to ascertain whether this candidate deserved a second look.

If the candidate came back in for a second interview, the hiring manager would dig a bit deeper and make sure the candidate knew as much about the position and the company as he or she could. The hiring manager was always looking for a successful track record going back to high school, college and previous jobs. Lenny's organization knew that the best predictor of future success was a successful track record. If you have had success in one area, you will have a tendency to continue that success pattern.

If the candidate was still viewed as a potential fit and if the candidate still felt that he or she wanted to work for this company, the candidate would come back in for a round of interviews with the hiring manager and 4 or 5 others within the organization.

At lunch time, the potential candidate would be taken to lunch by someone who does the job he or she is applying for. That associate would allow the candidate to ask any question he or she wanted to ask without fear that this associate was going to share the questions with anyone.

Lenny the Leader knew that the longer a person spent time with the organization and the more he or she learned about the position and the company, that person would be able to make a better decision. Lenny's company would be able to minimize turnover with this process. Lenny never wanted the organization to lose people because an associate felt that the position or the company is not what he or she thought it was when they signed on.   Lenny wanted the candidates to know as much about the organization as the organization was going to know about the candidates.

He also knew that the potential recruit, if given enough time in the process, would have to actually be themselves. Lenny knew that one could fake some things for a one hour interview, but that it would be difficult for someone to fake it over an extended period of time.

Additionally, Lenny knew that this candidate being referred to him meant that this was the best candidate for the position out of several they interviewed. The organization's recruiting and hiring process did not allow for a candidate pool of only one. Any time you have only one candidate in your pool, that candidate will look good. However, that is when mistakes occur.

Lenny and his organization knew that turnover costs everyone money and that the key to a low turnover rate was in the hiring process. You minimize turnover with your hiring process.

Meanwhile down the road, Mike the Boss was about to interview someone to be his new Sales Manager. His last

Sales Manager had quit and Mike did not have a Succession Program to promote someone to fill the slot.

He also did not think anyone on his team was good enough to be the new Sales Manager. He knew about each existing sales rep's issues and why they weren't performing as well as they should. The previous Sales Manager had always told him all of the issues each of the reps had and Mike the Boss had never taken enough time to get to know any of the folks to see if the Sales Manager had assessed the folks correctly. He had never been out on calls or visited a customer with any of them.

He just knew there had to be better qualified Sales Managers who would relish the opportunity to work for his company. Anyone from the outside had to be better than who he had in the organization.

This was the only interview Mike had scheduled because this guy had an incredible resume with lots of experience. He could not believe this guy was available. He just knew he would not need to interview anyone else. He needed to fill the job quickly and this guy appeared to have the right stuff. He did not need more than one candidate as Mike the Boss felt that he could make anyone successful even if he never spent any time with them.

In the interview, Mike was impressed. The guy had polished shoes, was wearing an expensive suit, an expensive watch, and looked the part. He looked professional.

Mike the Boss spent the majority of the interview talking about himself and the job and asked the applicant very few questions. Mike spent more than 80% of the time talking about himself.

Had he asked some penetrating questions and continued to dig to find substance, he would have known immediately that this was one of those Permanent Potential people who look good on paper but never have produced results. He would have also found out that the reason the candidate was available is that he had been fired for sexual harassment at his last employer. He would have also found out that wasn't the first time that had happened. He had been fired previously on the same issue.

Mike just knew this was the guy who could take his business to the next level. Even though he knew very little information about this candidate, he had not interviewed any one else, and no one else in his organization had interviewed him, he offered him the job on the spot. The candidate accepted as he knew he was lucky that no one was questioning his resume.

Chapter 4

After a successful interview, Lenny the Leader headed back to his office to conduct a performance review for one of his direct reports. Lenny's organization conducted formal performance reviews at mid-year and year-end.

Lenny's organization didn't just wait until mid-year to coach and provide feedback on performance. Lenny never wanted the review process and feedback to be a surprise.

Feedback was done regularly and consistently through-out the year. Good work was recognized and if there were performance issues, they were pointed out immediately with appropriate coaching to assist in performance improvement. If the needed improvement could not be attained, Lenny and the managing associates would take action. Sometimes that meant helping that individual find the right job for him or her within the organization if the individual was seen as someone who perhaps had been in the wrong position. Sometimes that meant terminating the individual once enough time and coaching had occurred to see if the individual could improve but unfortunately performance did not improve.

Lenny knew that the standard of performance becomes the performance of your weakest performer. That can tell an organization that this is the standard that the organization will tolerate.

He also knew that the organization watches how he handles performance issues. He knew that the people know who is carrying their weight and doing a good job and who isn't it. If he doesn't address performance issues the team can feel betrayed as that person is letting the team down. They will be disappointed in Lenny if he doesn't handle the issue and it can have a huge impact on the company's productivity.

Lenny opened the file for the associate about to be reviewed and read the information prior to discussing with the associate. The review would highlight the goals the associate and Lenny had agreed upon at the start of the year. He reviewed the bench marks for objectively measuring the progress or the attainment of the goal. He also reviewed the employee's self-assessment and reviewed the 360° feedback that he had received for the associate.

Lenny the Leader had implemented a 360° process some time back based on his experience at a prior company. After receiving candid feedback from associates on a survey of the associates, that company implemented a 360° review process. At that previous company he would see several notes from the associates that read, "If I could do my boss's review, he or she would never receive another promotion."

Lenny knew that there had been a lot of managers at that company who "managed up" quite well but were not so good at managing their reports or across the organization. He usually found that they were atrocious at customer relationships as well.

Their key to job security was that they could manage up well and did everything in their power to control and keep their reports from ever having an opportunity to visit with senior leadership. Any visits with senior leadership were carefully orchestrated and coached by the "managing-up" managers.

Lenny wanted to make sure he identified any of those "managing-up" managers as soon as possible and to get rid of that behavior. He knew that he would never be able to have a growing organization with those folks leading the organization. They stifle growth and run highly talented individuals out of the company in order to protect themselves.

Obviously, that is very misguided as the mark of a good leader is how many of your people develop into top-flight talent. "Managing-up" managers don't care about that though. They care about themselves. They also have a tendency to try to sabotage the careers of other high potential colleagues on the same level in order to eliminate competition for the "managing-up" managers.

The 360° Review feedback came from the Managing Associate's direct reports as well as team members across the organization they worked with in order to make sure that the folks were all working together well. The feedback also included customer input whenever possible.

Lenny felt his current organization was free of those "managing-up" managers but he still learned a lot about his people with the feedback he received. He was able to identify potential communication or other issues with his Managing Associates.

Lenny's organization also did not force rank performance into segments. He had worked with a company that forced managers to rank no more than 15% of the employees as Exceeds

Exceptions, no more than 70% as Meets Expectations, and a minimum of 15% as Does Not Meets. Their theory was that you always had a bottom tier of employees and you either needed them to get to Meets or Exceeds or to leave the organization so you could raise the performance bar.

However, the theory fell apart in actual practice. Many of the managers would not deal with their performance issues until review time to make sure they "saved" poor performing employees to make their percentages. A well run company always deals with performance issues on a timely basis and terminate employees when they should be terminated.

If a manager has performance managed his or her reports appropriately, the Does Not Meet Employees had already been terminated or in new positions that matched their skills better. That manager, who had managed appropriately, was punished for doing what a good manager should do, performance manage and deal with issues immediately rather than wait until the end of the year. That manager was actually punished at review time because he or she had to place a Does Not Meet on an individual who did not deserve that classification. Lenny knew that was an incredible example of "No good deed shall go unpunished."

That system ran off some good talent at the manager level as well as the employee level. That was one key reason Lenny left that company as well.

Lenny met with the Managing Associate and they had a very good two-way communication session about the associate's performance as well as long term career aspirations. Lenny always wanted to make sure he knew his reports' aspirations so that they could put plans in place to help that associate attain the career he or she wanted. At the end of the session, Lenny indicated to the associate that he would write the performance review and allow the employee to review prior to signing and add any comments the employee wanted to add.

Meanwhile, Mike the Manager headed off to his office as he too had performance reviews to do. Unlike Lenny the Leader, he was totally unprepared for the review. He had spent no time reviewing 360° information because he did not believe in the process. As a matter of fact, he did not like doing performance reviews as he thought they were a waste of his valuable time. If he had it his way no one would receive a performance review. In many situations he just did not do a review unless the employee forced the issue.

Mike also did not do a lot of coaching and providing feedback along the way. His employees would always go into the meetings without any idea what surprises might be in store for them. They also had not set up a performance plan at the beginning of the year to serve as their goals as Mike did not believe in them and did not want to have to spend time on those discussions.

Mike conducted the review with him doing almost all of the talking. There was no opportunity for the employee to provide feedback or question any of the feedback he or she would be receiving. There were also plenty of surprises on situations that had never been brought up before. The employee always felt that if something had been an issue surely Mike the Boss would have said something right then.

Unfortunately, Mike subscribed to the "gotcha" theory. He would just write notes in the file and at review time, bring up issues in a "gotcha" style.

In the rare circumstances that Mike had provided feedback when something first occurred it was usually in front of people and never in private. (Lenny always corrected behavior in private...never in public) Mike would criticize the person and not the behavior indicating things like "you are so stupid!" He did not talk about the behavior that wasn't working. He personalized it!

At the end of the session, Mike would ask the employee, "You don't want me to write this up, do you? I am just going to put some notes in your file."

Unless the employee specifically said that he or she wanted a written copy, Mike never formalized the reviews. The employee also usually did not call his hand on that as to do so would be to make him angry and no one wanted that to happen. Mike had been known to fire people when he was angry at them. To the employee, it just wasn't worth it.

There was no discussion of career aspirations for the employee. Mike the Boss felt that his people should be happy just having a job and a paycheck and it was not his job to make sure people could feel like they could attain higher levels.

Needless to say, employees left their performance reviews with Mike angry, disillusioned and with plans to find another job.

CHAPTER 5

At the end of their review session, Lenny's Managing Associate asked Lenny if he had a few minutes to talk about a Customer Service Rep situation he needed to deal with. The Managing Associate indicated to Lenny that he had a Customer Service Rep that had scored some business in a company contest that should not have counted by the contest rules. That scoring allowed the Customer Service Rep to win the contest. The reward for winning was a $100 gift check.

The Customer Service Rep was also their very best Customer Service Rep who always had achieved more than the other reps. Lenny asked the managing associate had they determined that it was indeed cheating and not just a simple mistake that could be corrected.

The Managing Associate explained that it was not a mistake and the Customer Service Rep knew he had cheated. It was a willful act in order to win the contest.

Lenny asked the Managing Associate how he was going to handle the situation. The Managing Associate replied that he was going to fire the Customer Rep.

The Managing Associate knew the organization would not and could not tolerate cheating. The fact that the Customer Rep was the best performing Customer Rep did not enter the decision process. You take action no matter who the offender is. It could be your best rep or your worst rep. It does not matter.

The Managing Associate operated with core values and principles. His decision was easy. He knew what he had to do.

The rest of the organization knew this rep had cheated. They were watching to see if the Managing Associate's actions mirrored what he had always said. No cheating allowed. If you cheat you are gone.

Lenny agreed with the Managing Associate and thanked him for letting him know. He also complimented him for being true to his values and principles.

Lenny knew that the rest of the organization would take notice and know that they worked for a company where they stood by their word and their values. The company values can never be viewed as elastic where they can be stretched. Ethics and honesty cannot be molded like play dough for a particular situation.

In dealing with these kinds of issues, one needed to cut right to the heart of the issue. It does not matter if it is only $100 or that it is your best rep who cheated. That should not even enter the decision process.

Meanwhile down the road, Mike the Boss had a bit of a different dilemma. He found out his best sales rep had cheated a customer on purpose in order to make more money. Mike did not want to fire the rep. It was his best rep.

The rest of the organization knew about the cheating and they were all watching how Mike the Boss handled the situation. Mike defused the issue with the customer refunding the overcharge, but then just assigned another rep to the account as the customer did not want to see the best rep ever again. The customer was expecting that Mike would fire the rep.

Mike did not do that. He just assigned a new rep to the account.

He also charged the rep back the overage he had received on his commissions but that was all the action he took. After all, this was his best rep so he made excuses for him.

Mike the Boss managed by Principals and not Principles. If that had been his worst rep, that rep would have been fired.

The rest of the organization saw that the best rep kept his job. They now trusted the organization even less.

The other reps knew if they ever wanted to be the best rep, they were going to have to cheat. Many indicated if that is how the game is played, that is how I will play the game. Others felt a need to leave so more turnover occurred.

Mike the Boss lost a great opportunity to send the right message to his organization and to insure he had the appropriate behavior at all times within the organization if he would have fired the rep. Instead he signaled to the organization that anything goes which was totally the wrong message to send.

CHAPTER 6

Lenny the Leader then left the building with a Sales Rep to see one of their best customers. Lenny absolutely loved going out with the reps and seeing prospects and customers.

He not only received first hand information from customers about what his competition was doing, he had a chance to engage in conversations with the reps to see how the company was doing and what they could do better. It was a great time for what some companies would call a skip level discussion where the associate's actual immediate supervisor isn't around during the discussion.

Lenny's organization did not need a formal skip level discussion program as is needed in some companies to insure it happens. It is a matter of course at Lenny's company.

The particular company that they were visiting was a very big customer who had been spending a lot of money with Lenny's organization. Lenny already knew the people and had visited with them regularly. If there were ever any issues or problems Lenny's organization always listened and resolved the issues.

This company was currently experiencing some lean times. They were asking for a break on the price they were paying Lenny's organization. Lenny knew they would not be asking for a break if they really did not need the money as they had always paid the price that Lenny's organization asked them to pay.

This company had also been recently acquired by another company and the parent company was asking them to shop the business. They were demanding reduced costs. Lenny knew they had a very good relationship with the customer.

The customer told Lenny that she did not want to shop the business but if she did not reduce the costs, the parent company would take action. She had no choice but to ask for a break.

Lenny told her how much he could reduce the cost. The customer agreed with the price and indicated that as a result she was not going to shop the business. She did not want to switch to another company.

Lenny was not forced to cut even more margin in a competitive bid because he and his company had treated this customer well and they had built a relationship based on trust and mutual respect. The relationship had been built on a win-win basis and would remain in place.

Mike the Boss was on his way over to this account as well. This account was spending a lot of money with Mike the Boss' company. Unfortunately, they had never met Mike the Boss so there was no real relationship. At the same time, Mike the Boss' company had continued to turn over the rep that called on this account so there was not even a loyalty at the rep level.

This company had been a customer of Mike the Boss' company for 7 years. The only person from Mike the Boss' company that the customer had met was whatever rep was working their account that year.

The rep had originally told Mike that the customer was going to shop the business and that they could lose the account. Mike was furious at the rep and indicated to the rep there was no way they were going to cut their price and the rep needed to do what he needed to do to keep the business. He had an internal meeting that was more important at the same time as the proposed meeting and to let him know if the rep could not handle this. He told the rep that if the rep could not handle the situation he would find a rep that could. He also said make sure you don't lose this account.

Mike was more internally focused than externally focused which is a recipe for having a dying company. Mike the Boss never visited with customers unless forced to do so.

The rep reported back that the account was not happy and that they were indeed going to shop it. The rep suggested another meeting time that would not interfere with Mike's internal meetings.

Mike was outraged at the rep and the situation, but decided that they would mount an all out effort to keep this account. He arranged for all of the top Senior Managers in the organization to go see this customer with Mike. They had never seen the customer before this.

They went to the meeting and Mike the Boss told them how much his company valued their business. He said to them "you mean so much to us that I have brought my entire Senior Management Team with me to show you how much we appreciate your business."

The customer asked, "If you value our business so much how come you have never been to see us? You only came to see us since we have threatened to shop this business. We have spent a lot of money with your organization through the years and now you send all of your top people out here to tell us how much you love us?"

The customer then said that the meeting was over and that they were giving the business to someone else. Mike's internal focus was the culprit. He had needed to spend time visiting customers and had never done so.

Mike spun a message to his organization that the competitor dramatically reduced their price and to such extent that there was no way they could match it. The rep knew that was not true and left the organization. The rest of the organization also knew what really happened.

CHAPTER 7

Lenny went from the meeting with the customer to a meeting with a new prospect with the Sales Rep. This was a potentially large customer who had a need for Lenny's company's services.

It did not take long for Lenny to find out that in order to accommodate this customer his company would have to make an exception to how they normally process business. Lenny's company would have to "engineer" a system fix that would require several manual interventions each month and each one of those could become messy.

The manual interventions could also cause the system to make errors in other customers' orders. Lenny also knew that manual interventions could result in additional human errors as a manual intervention requires someone to intervene.

Lenny began to realize that he would be trying to place a square peg in a round hole by accepting this business. He knew that they could find a way to make the exception but in doing so, there was a risk of not only being unable to keep this customer happy but it could have an impact on other customers' business. He also knew that he would have to charge the customer more in order to do this profitably. He could eat the additional cost but that would mean accepting business with very little chance of this customer's business being profitable for his company.

Lenny knew he had to walk away from the business. He told the customer, "We are not the company for you. My company would have to do this business manually outside of our regular process. You would end up not being happy with us as we could make mistakes along the way and we would have to charge you more. There are other companies who meet your needs without a manual intervention."

The customer knew that there were other companies who could meet their needs but had heard good things about Lenny's company and had hoped to do business with his company. However, the customer respected the fact that Lenny knew that his company could not really meet his needs.

He told Lenny that he really appreciated his honesty and his candor. Perhaps one day in the future they would have a need that Lenny's company could match.

On the way to the car Lenny asked the Sales Rep if the sales rep understood why he had to make that call. The

Sales Rep acknowledged that while that was a large commission that he wanted, he also knew that as a Rep he had a duty to be concerned about the profitability of the company and that he was hoping to be with the company for a long time. Short term gain is not worth long term pain.

Lenny knew that the rep was on board and he felt he would hear that same thing from anyone he worked with. The reps and everyone's compensation plans aligned with the company's profit attainment. That meant everyone would be in alignment about the need for profitable revenue growth and not just revenue growth.

Lenny also knew that an exception for this company could make sense. They could find a way to make it work. Good company, sizable revenue. He knew though, that when you look at any one exception, it could be a good business decision. However, when you look at 500 of those good exception business decisions over time, you can have chaos in your operation. Lenny had once worked for a company where almost 50% of the business was done as an exception process from the normal process. There were all kinds of customer issues as a result.

Meanwhile, Mike the Boss was meeting with a potential new customer down the road. After his disappointment in losing the previous account, he really wanted this business. Unfortunately, this business was going to require an exception.

That was Ok for Mike the Boss. He had rarely met an exception he didn't want to do. Mike always figured that business was business and he did not care if it could result in an unhappy customer down the road. His theory was let's get the business in the door and then we will worry about what we have to do to satisfy the customer. That drove his people crazy.

They knew that Mike would do anything for a sale. They knew that he would figure out later if it was going to be profitable or not.

Mike the Boss figured it was up to the people he was paying to figure out all of the mechanics necessary. They needed every order they could get and he did not care if the organization had to run around like chickens with their heads cut off trying to deliver the next to impossible.

The employees knew it was a no-win situation for them. Even if they were successful at finding a way to make the exception work, Mike would never tell them that they had done a good job. He just felt that was their job, they were getting paid, and the employees should be grateful that they had a job and a paycheck.

Mike the Boss' Operations employees knew that over half of their business was an exception. That meant that the exception was the norm. They also knew that as a company they would never grow and prosper as they were losing a customer as fast as they would gain one.

Everyone knew that retaining an existing customer was more profitable than starting up with a new one, but Mike did not pay attention to that. He would just get angry when someone would come to him and tell him how much money it was costing him to do these exceptions. He did not want to hear any bad news. He had even been known to fire people who told him they should not take a customer.

Mike told the customer that they would do a terrific job for him. The customer hesitated briefly so Mike decided to go one more step.

Mike the Boss said to the prospective customer, if I reduce my price by 10% will you give me the order today? He did not need to cut the price. If he had known his competition very well he would have known that his organization was probably the only one who would take the business the way the customer wanted. He had already reduced his margins by agreeing to the exception and rather than probe to find out what the real hesitancy was he just responded with the only way he knew...cut the price.

The customer was eager to sign that day. He was getting what he wanted and at a 10% lower price that he never even requested.

The rep that was with Mike was appalled. He knew what was going to happen next. As the rep for the account the 10% was going to come out of his commissions. Mike would reason that as a rep I just sold this for you and for us to take this business to help you out Mr. Rep, we are going to make less money. Mr. Rep, you have to share in that reduction and you should be grateful that I am paying you anything on a sale I just made for you.

The rep also knew the Operations people and the Finance people were going to be unhappy about this deal. He was going to have to hear how lousy this deal was forever as they certainly weren't going to whine about it to Mike. No, he knew it would be his fault when all was said and done.

The rep made a decision that Mike would never go out on a call with him again, no matter what. He also decided to polish his resume and begin a hunt for a new opportunity. He had zero respect for Mike the Boss

CHAPTER 8

Lenny headed back to the office to meet with the financial folks to review the quarterly numbers. It was time to release the numbers to the public and he needed to be up to speed with everything prior to the investor conference call.

When Lenny walked into the room he could tell the financial folks were a bit concerned about the quarterly results. Their heads were down and a couple of them did not want to look up.

Lenny asked them what was going on. They indicated to him that while the firm had hit their revenue, expenses and profit goal for the quarter, the numbers were not going to please the analysts who regularly covered their company.

Those analysts were accustomed to the company exceeding the quarterly targets and the numbers barely hit the targets. The analysts had projected 10% more for the quarter than Lenny and the other Senior Managers of the firm had targeted. The stock price was going to suffer as soon as the results were released.

Lenny just said the numbers are the numbers and we run this business for long term success. We are not running this business for the analysts and the financial companies.

Lenny continued that the company was making long term decisions and not quarterly decisions and if our company is fundamentally strong, our stockholders will be rewarded by our consistent profit. He was not going to worry that one quarter did not match the expectations of the stock analysts.

He continued by reminding folks that if they were meeting the expectations of the customers, the company would be successful. Lenny indicated that he would cover that on the conference call.

He told everyone to relax. If the stock went down, it would only be temporary. The stock would come right back up.

Having said that and knowing that the company had consistently exceeded the expectations of the analysts, he asked if there was a reason that the numbers were just at goal versus 10-15% higher than the analysts were expecting. He asked what happened as at the mid-quarter projections, the company was projecting to exceed the target by a fairly sizable margin.

The Chief Financial Officer said that it was not anything major. The local economy was in a downturn and some of their customers were taking longer to pay than normal.

She indicated that their accounts receivables were higher than normal at quarter end. A lot of revenue would move into the next quarter.

The Senior Leader of the Customer Service area indicated that they had called a lot of the customers to make sure all was Ok and they all indicated they simply had customers paying them late as they had temporary cash flow issues. There was no long term issue that they could see.

Lenny indicated he was not worried and expected that any dip in the stock price would be because of the economic conditions and not the performance of the company. He continued by saying the company was not going to react and do anything differently. Their business formula was working and they just needed to continue with their plans.

Meanwhile down the road, Mike the Boss headed into his quarterly results meeting and saw his financial people with their heads down as well. Mike immediately said, "What the heck is going on? Don't be giving me any bad news. We need a big quarter."

What Mike did not say out loud but was thinking was that he had stock options he could exercise after the numbers were released and he did not want the stock price to go down. Plus he did not need the "heat" he was going to feel from the board of directors for the stock price going south.

Mike just asked, "What are the numbers for the quarter?"

The Chief Financial Officer said, "We are under the goal by 10% and missed the analysts projection by 20%."

Mike just shook his head and yelled, "That is freaking unacceptable. You must have counted something incorrectly. Go back and recalculate the numbers. I am not going to sign off on a report that says we missed the targets. My expectation is the same as the analysts. We hit their projection."

When one of the financial folks tried to get Mike to understand they had already checked and rechecked the numbers, he interrupted him and said, "You must not like your job very much because if we don't recalculate the numbers and show that we hit the analysts projections, I am firing some people and getting some financial people in here who understand our business better and who know how to make sure we hit numbers each quarter."

Mike continued and said that the meeting was over and to find him once they had corrected their errors and the numbers were finally accurate. With that he cursed and walked out of the meeting slamming the door as he left.

CHAPTER 9

Lenny then had a meeting set up with the people developing the company's business plan for the following year. There were associates from every area of the company participating as representatives of their various areas.

Lenny had appointed two people to drive the entire process. Those two associates had excellent facilitating skills and were two of the individuals in the company that had been identified as having high potential. Driving the planning process was a great way to challenge the individuals and also to continue their development within the organization.

Those two took this project on as their full time job for this year's planning process. Someone else was performing the duties of their normal positions so they could focus full-time on pulling next year's plan together.

Lenny knew that the "tyranny of the urgent" could keep key people from doing their very best on the planning process if they had to be the ones pulling the final plan together. The process of pulling every department's plans together could keep them from performing their normal roles.

The "tyranny of the urgent" is all of those phone calls that seem urgent that need to be returned. They are also last minute issues that need a sign-off. Lenny did not want to jeopardize the smooth day-to-day operations of his organization by having everyone pulled in a lot of different directions.

The planning process belonged to these two individuals who would meet with the various Senior Managers and the key people in each of their organizations to identify the key external opportunities for the organization as well as the key external threats the company faced. They also identified the internal strengths and weaknesses of the organization.

The two planners also collected the initial passes of the departments' plans on how they would attack the opportunities and minimize or eliminate the threats the departments could face. They would also identify the potential obstacles to being able to address an opportunity to the appropriate level. Sometimes those obstacles were external and sometimes they were internal.

The two planners would bring all of this together and the Senior Leaders of the organization along with some of their key people would discuss and rank-order the opportunities. Once agreement was met on the order, each department would work on what they needed to do to assist the company in achieving that opportunity.

Each department would work on their part of the plan to identify the action steps and the resources they needed to accomplish their part of the plan. They would all work with the finance area to determine the cost for what they needed to accomplish the priority.

The two planners would oversee all of these steps. They made sure deadlines were hit. They also made sure that each department thought about the impact of their proposed actions on the other departments so that communication between departments continued. They also participated in the discussions each department was having within their organization to understand what each area needed and where they were headed.

Each department would roll their plans up to the two planners and the two planners would consolidate the various plans. They would have a regular meeting with Lenny the Leader to keep him posted on where everyone was in the process and identify any problem areas on the horizon.

During those meetings, if Lenny saw something he thought needed to go in a different direction or if he had questions, he would either task the two planners with relaying the message to the Senior Leaders or he would indicate that he wanted to talk with that particular Senior Leader first.

Once all the input was gathered and an initial pass at the plan was ready to roll, the two planners met with Lenny and the Senior Leaders to discuss the plans and make sure that their plan was a go or if it needed to be refined. The entire Senior Leadership team would participate in the discussions and reach agreement on the final plan.

Once the plans were finished, there would be a communication process outlined. The Senior Leaders would communicate with each of their various departments the overall plan and their department's role in attaining that plan.   Since the Senior Leaders had involved the key people in their departments in the planning process there were very few surprises for a particular area. They also had buy-in as the key people in those areas had helped design their department's strategies and actions.

The plans would be in writing along with the goals of the organization for the year.   Lenny the Leader would also hold a meeting with all of the employees to give the vision for the company for the following year and to outline the major initiatives of the plan. He would take questions and input from the associates.

Lenny knew that if the associates knew where you wanted them to go, they would take you there. He thought about it like a trip across country. If you just started driving your car toward the other coast, you could ultimately get there by continually stopping and asking for directions. However, if you had a Map or a GPS, you would not waste time stopping for directions. You would get there much faster. That was why every employee needed to know the plan. They needed to know where they were headed on next year's journey.

The various departments would take the overall plan and design their departments' plans and objectives for the year. That would constitute the framework for each employee's performance plan.

The Finance and Human Resource folks would take the plan and design the compensation plans for incentives and bonuses for the employees. The compensation and incentives always had to be aligned with the company's goals and plans. There was alignment throughout the organization.

Lenny knew that if the compensation plans were aligned with the corporation goals, there would be no resentment of a sales rep that was making a lot of money as that sales rep was making the company a lot of money. Everyone in the organization was being paid for the same objectives.

You never wanted to be in a situation where someone's direct report's compensation paid them for results that were in conflict with how the supervising associate was being paid. If you have alignment throughout the organization, every one is marching in the same direction.

The plans just did not get placed in a file or on a shelf to gather dust. They were reviewed and regular reports on how the company was progressing toward attaining those goals for the year were communicated to all employees. There was alignment and everyone was pursuing the same objectives.

Meanwhile, down the road, Mike the Boss, was taking a few minutes in his office designing next year's plan and objectives. Mike did not believe he needed to involve his people in designing the plans for the following year. He felt he knew best.

He used a top down approach. He thought he could just outline the plan himself and just tell people what they needed to accomplish for the company. He did not want to waste a lot of time meeting with people who did not really understand that you just had to work a bit harder and focus better on their jobs to grow the organization. Mike the Boss just thought you could just sell more business and the profits would fall into place.

Mike did not believe in a budgeting process. He just took this year's budget and added 10% to everything.

He also just picked a number that felt good to him for the revenue target and the sales numbers. He was a firm believer if you gave people a number they would find a way to hit it.

He truly felt you could just sell your
way to greatness.

CHAPTER 10

After his meeting with the two planners, Lenny walked with them to their next meeting. Lenny was spending time with the folks in the organization who were in their Succession Management Program.

He used this as an opportunity to get to know the people identified as the future leaders of the organization. He wanted to know them and to be in a position to discuss the future leaders' opportunities with each of their sponsoring Senior Leaders.

At the same time, Lenny wanted to allow them to ask him questions and to learn some of the lessons he had to learn the hard way in a previous organization. He had learned his lessons the hard way as in the previous organization he worked with he was appointed a manager without having any formal training at all.

Lenny knew that there were a lot of companies that were like that. They did not invest in their leadership team and as a result they many times had bad managers and leaders. The practice was just to promote someone who had been around a long time or someone who was doing a good job in their current role. Many times that meant that not only did you get a poor manager, you lost a good performer so you took a double hit. In reality it was a lot more than just a double hit as those bad managers had higher turnover than other managers.

Lenny knew that the primary reason that people will leave your organization is because they feel they have a bad manager. It is not for more money or a better opportunity. It is having a lousy boss.

In those organizations without Succession Management Programs there was usually a standard joke that would spread around the organization. "Yesterday he or she could not even spell Manager, and now he or she are one."

Lenny also knew that employees who feel they can continue increasing their roles and learning feel more valued and don't need to look for other opportunities. He knew that the message that promoting from within sent was incredibly valuable to the associates.

He also recognized that he never knew what he would get if he had to recruit someone from outside the organization to fill a leadership role. His company did a good job in the screening process but still mistakes could happen.

Lenny also wanted to make sure that he had people heading into a leadership role who would use their power for good and not for evil. A leader in an organization has position power. That power is important in getting things done in an organization but Lenny had seen too many leaders at a previous company use their powers for evil and not for good.

Lenny also knew that people were either growing or they were dying. If you are not growing, you are just getting older and that will ultimately mean death. The Succession Management Program allows people to continue to grow.

An added bonus in having a Succession Management Program is that the sponsoring Senior Leaders also sharpened their skills by their mentoring of these future leaders. They wanted to make sure that they were setting the right example.

Lenny would start their session by asking them what they had been working on in their development program and what they were learning. He also welcomed questions about his leadership practices and about the direction of the company. He also welcomed any input on new ideas or things the company could do better.

One of the future leaders asked him about his previous experiences and if he had any good role models at the leadership level. Lenny smiled and indicated he had some role models who were good at leading and he had some who were atrocious at it.

He added though that he learned just as much from the bad leaders as the good ones. He said that even a bad leader can be a great example. In many cases the bad leadership behavior jumps out at you as an example even more so than the good behavior. He learned what not to do from the bad leaders.

Lenny enjoyed these sessions with these future leaders. It would sometimes remind him that he himself needed to be careful. Sometimes things work so well we stop doing them. Not intentionally, it just happens.

Lenny knew that in a person's development in a particular role, you usually have four stages of development:

1. Unconsciously Incompetent where you have no idea what you are doing and have no idea

how bad you are screwing up or
how little you know.
2. Consciously Incompetent where
you realize you are screwing up
and how little you know.
3. Consciously Competent where
you know how to do the role and
you are performing it well.
4. Unconsciously Competent where
the activity is a habit and you
are performing the role well and
you don't think about what you
are doing.

At that 4th stage is when one has to be
careful. At this stage, Lenny knew that
you could end up not paying attention
to your actions so much that you
become unconsciously incompetent
again. In other words, it worked so
well I stopped doing it.

Meeting with the Succession
Management people allowed him to
really think about what he needed to

do on a day to day basis. Lenny knew that it is what you do everyday that counts for a leader.

Lenny also believed in having everyone in the organization have a developmental area in their performance plan. Everyone needed to continue to grow if the organization as well as the people in the organization were going to survive and prosper.

The pace of change is so great and phenomenal that if one doesn't keep growing, the individual will get left behind. It will also mean the company will get left behind.

Lenny remembered people he had worked with early in his career who were superstars. They outperformed every one else by large margins. Unfortunately, many of them focused so much on the day to day results that they did not attempt to keep growing and learning. As a result, the organization grew right past them and they became average performing employees at best.

Lenny not only required all of the associates to have a personal development plan as part of their performance plan, he also required one for himself. He was a big believer in a now famous John Wooden quote, "It is what you learn after you know it all that counts!"

Meanwhile down the road, Mike the Boss was meeting with one of the employees who was trying to get Mike to approve a Talent Development Program where the organization could identify high potential talent and help them develop with different types of training courses or college courses.

The employee soon realized he had no chance of getting this done. Mike was either looking out the window, or taking a phone call or Mike would become distracted by a message coming in on his BlackBerry.

You see Mike had little interest in development plans especially for managers. He felt people should just do their jobs, be grateful they have jobs, and if they want to learn new things, go somewhere else or do it on their own time and not his time when he was paying them. After all, he had never received any training and he turned out great. They all needed to "Man up" and stop making excuses. It was their responsibility to continue to grow and the company should not have anything to do with that.

CHAPTER 11

Lenny's organization now had a regularly scheduled meeting for all employees as the day was beginning to come to a close. At least once a month Lenny would address the organization in order to communicate key messages, provide an update on how the company was doing toward attaining their current year plan, recognize exceptional performance by the associates and celebrate accomplishments of the organization.

The sessions also allowed all of the employees to ask questions of Lenny or any of the other leaders of the organization anything that was on their mind. Lenny loved these sessions and the questions or input he received during them.

The organization made sure that these meetings were not creating unnecessary interruptions in customer service levels as some of the employees needed to stay on the job in order to provide the excellent service their customers had come to expect. They knew when the call volumes were the lowest so they scheduled the meetings at that time. They would keep a few people at their desks to take calls from the customers. The associates would rotate each month who would attend the meetings and who would stay at the desks.

Lenny loved having these sessions. He knew that communication was occurring at all times in the organization but he knew that an organization that does not hear from its leadership begins to craft and spin messages on their own. He was a firm believer in open and frequent communication.

He also knew that if he did not meet with the group and only communicated by memo or email, the organization would read the white print and not the black print. He did not want people reading between the lines. He wanted everyone to know what was occurring in the organization.

In the meetings, he would speak from a platform but that was to make sure everyone could see him. He did not have a podium. He walked around the stage and looked at everyone as he spoke.

He worked from notes and did not read a message. He spoke from his heart when he talked about the company, its mission, its accomplishments as well as the exceptional performance of his people.

Lenny knew that as the leader he needed to create the vision for the organization. He knew he needed to continuously restate that vision and update people regularly on how the company was doing versus that vision.

He also knew that if the organization knew where they were headed, they would find ways to take the company there. He also knew that they needed to celebrate their victories along the way.

Lenny made sure that when they were doing the question and answer session that if there was a question better handled by another Senior Leader, he called on that Senior Leader to answer that question. He was not concerned about making sure he had all of the answers. The meeting was not about Lenny or for Lenny. It was for the people. Lenny could get his ego out of the way in order to make sure his

Senior Leaders were getting the recognition for their valuable contributions as well as to insure the employees were not getting any mixed messages if Lenny might miss a detail or two.

Lenny also knew that the associates would be watching his body language as much as listening to his message in this session. Lenny never ever folded his arms in his meetings or in his interactions with people. He knew that sent a message that he was not open to the other person's idea or feedback or did not believe the person. He never ever folded his arms.

He had once seen the CEO of a former company he worked with fold his arms in a meeting of 100 of the top leaders of the company. The company had just gone through a merger, and the CEO was new to many of them in the room.   The company Lenny had worked with had basically been acquired by this new CEO's company. While it was conveniently called a merger there was no mistake this CEO's company had swallowed the company Lenny was with and had designs on getting rid of many of the people from the company they had acquired.

This CEO not only folded his arms at one of the questions, he folded his arms every time a woman asked a question. He sent a message loud and clear who he was at that moment.

He would also respond to a question by anyone coming from his original company that was a good question. He never said that to a question from anyone working at the company they bought.

Lenny had seen what that particular meeting did to the morale of the leadership group as well as the rest of the organization. Valuable talent that was needed to insure the success of the merged company left as quickly as they could. (Especially bright and talented women leaders) The company was never the same. The company lost tremendous market share and the stock price fell dramatically.

Lenny also made sure there was plenty of time for people to ask their questions and to discuss the answers. He had seen that same leader pontificate for so long that the entire question and answer time would be used for two or three questions. It seemed to the organization that the leader felt if he was talking no one could ask him the tough question he did not want to answer.

Lenny invited questions and discussions. Everyone felt comfortable asking the question and everyone felt that Lenny cared what they thought. That was because Lenny did care and he was real.

When Lenny and the other Senior Leaders recognized the organization for outstanding performance, they made sure that the performance by individuals or departments were indeed outstanding and that they were not just recognizing ordinary performance. Lenny felt that an organization would receive exactly what the organization expected to receive.

As a result, the company needed to make sure that the exceptional, outstanding performance they recognized was indeed exceptional. If the celebration and recognition was for ordinary results, you would continue receiving ordinary results. The company needed to set a high bar and Lenny was continually raising the expectations of performance.

People left those meetings with smiles on their faces. They were happy to work at a place where the energy and excitement was contagious. Celebrating the victories and the recognition that comes with good performance was a big part of creating that energy and excitement.

They loved working for an organization that not only communicated the vision but also kept them informed along the way about how the organization was doing. They also loved working for an organization where open communication was valued.

Mike the Boss only had those all employee meetings when something was wrong. He had those "get to know your higher power" meetings when things were in the ditch.

Mike the Boss thought that fear and intimidation was the best motivator. He felt the organization needed to see him angry in order to make progress.

He did everything just the opposite of Lenny. He would fold his arms. He would laugh and sneer at folks who asked what he thought was a stupid question.

He would say that was a stupid question and who do you report to? He wanted to ridicule the employee's immediate supervisor as well for the employee asking such a stupid question.

He also shot the messenger. If an employee brought up bad news, he was "shot" and made to look stupid.

He did all of this in front of all of the employees. The result is that no one ever wanted to ask any questions or to provide any feedback. The meetings ended up with just Mike the Boss pontificating about what was wrong and if performance did not change, people would be fired.

Mike would also not allow anyone to miss his meetings. He felt that his meeting was too important for anyone to miss and that the customers could just leave a voice mail. Mike would ask his direct reports to explain why anyone was missing from the meeting.

The employees just laughed when Mike scheduled a meeting. They knew they were in for a tirade of how bad they were and they were now so used to it that they just laughed about Mike. They had no respect for him.

CHAPTER 12

Lenny left the meeting with his employees and headed back to his office. It had been a great day but also a long one. However, being with the people he worked with always energized him.

He had one more item on his agenda for the day, a conference call with the network of independent contractors who sold products for them nationally. Employing independent contractors was different than having employees.

Independent contractors usually had some different motivators than an employee. They wanted to be independent for a reason. They did not like having anyone structure and manage their activity and they really liked being able to come and go as they pleased. They were fiercely protective of their freedom.

An employer also has to be careful when dealing with independent contractors. If the employer exercises too much control, the IRS could rule that the independent contractor is an employee.

Generally, an employer withholds income taxes, withholds and pays Social Security and Medicare taxes, and pays unemployment tax on wages paid to employees. You do not generally have to withhold or pay any taxes on payments to independent contractors.

In other words, if an independent contractor is actually treated like an employee, the employer is going to have increased expenses. In some circumstances that could mean the independent contractor would have to be included in the company Pension Plan which could really drive up costs.

While the IRS guidelines listed several items that an organization needed to avoid to having an independent contractor ruled an employee, in a nutshell, Lenny's organization could not manage their activity. Lenny's organization could not require activity reports nor could they make them attend these conference calls. Lenny's organization could only evaluate their performance on actual results.

Having independent contractors was a win-win for Lenny's organization and the independent contractors. Lenny's organization saved money on employee benefit costs and the independent contractors could keep the freedoms they wanted.

Lenny had seen his former company and its leaders really struggle working with independent contractors. That is because the organization's leaders were primarily "Command and Control" types of leaders. They wanted to treat these folks as employees so they could use the "Stick" portion of the "Stick and Carrot" theory of motivating people.

Those leaders still wanted to tell the independent contractors what they wanted and to threaten them with being fired if they did not produce the activity necessary. They could care less about the IRS guidelines or what really motivated the independent contractor.

As a result, there was always a lot of turnover in the independent contractor networks at Lenny's former employer. That was not good for bringing in the profitable revenue they needed.

Additionally, the IRS was constantly challenging the former organization, threatening fines and suggesting they needed to treat these folks as employees. Also, many of the independent contractors who were dissatisfied not only left the organization, they also sued Lenny's former employer. The former company's leaders were constantly in court.

Lenny did not have those issues with his current organization's network. His independent contractors respected him and voluntarily attended his meetings. They also voluntarily provided Lenny's organization with activity reports so that Lenny's company could accurately project sales in order to have the resources available to process the business. Without those reports, Lenny's organization could find they were scrambling at the last minute hiring people to process and service a large sale or a number of sales they were not expecting.

Lenny's organization's Independent Contractor Network respected him. They knew Lenny respected them and he listened to them. The network knew that Lenny always told them the truth and would always be candid. If there were problems brewing, he let them know.

Lenny also spent time pointing out to the contractors how they could work together better. He pointed out to them that the reason the organization would like to have the voluntary activity information is that it allowed his organization to serve their customers better. Lenny's organization could manage the work flow and be more responsive. The independent contractors would receive their commissions earlier if the organization could better manage the new business coming in the door.

The independent contractors also enjoyed attending Lenny's meeting. Not only did the independent contractors know Lenny would not waste their time just having a meeting, they knew Lenny made sure they covered items that would benefit the independent contractors and help the independent contractors make more money.

Lenny did not try to manage the independent contractors. He influenced them. He was a leader to the independent contractor network.

Meanwhile, Mike the manager was having a meeting with his employee who oversaw their independent contractor network. Mike thought he was too good to spend any time with the independent contractors. He did not respect them.

Given how he treated them, the independent contractors did not respect Mike at all either. They would only place an order with Mike's company if the product was clearly the very best or perhaps only option for the customer.

Mike was appalled that he could not obtain reports and fire these folks. He felt that if they were selling his products, he should be able to dictate how they sold the products and where. He also felt that he should be able to require them to give him reports.

Mike thought that network of independent contractors should be grateful that he was allowing them to sell his products. He thought he was doing them a favor.

Even bigger issues came into play if one of the independent contractors was competing with one of Mike's company's employees. Mike was known to personally get involved with the employee sales rep to try to defeat the independent contractor on the sale. Mike had also been in shouting matches with the independent contractors and had even hung up the phone on them in anger previously.

He was also responsible for the audit being conducted by the IRS to see if Mike's company's actions had created an employee relationship for the independent contractors. That could end up costing Mike's company a lot of money.

Additionally, Mike was responsible for several lawsuits the company had to deal with over improper terminations of some of the independent contractor's contracts. If an independent contractor crossed Mike or if Mike just did not care for the independent contractor, he forced the legal department to aggressively terminate their contracts.

The attorneys would caution Mike that they would be sued, but Mike did not care. He said let's see if they have a deep enough wallet to fund their attorney fees to take us to court. He did not feel that any of them would be able to financially sue them and if they did, it would be years before Mike's company would have to pay them anything as they could keep it tied up in courts for years.

Mike just did not care. He wanted that network to do business his way.

The meeting today with Mike's employee who was responsible for the independent contractor network was to review a meeting the employee had with the biggest producer for the independent contractor network. The independent contractor had been doing business with Mike's organization a long time and had this strange sense of loyalty to the organization in spite of Mike the Manager.

The top producing independent contractor had shared with Mike's employee the concerns the independent contractor network had about Mike's company. The concern centered on Mike's company's products becoming uncompetitive.

The network was also concerned about what they called the horrible service they and their customers were receiving from Mike the Manager's company. The constant turnover of employees meant there were always new people having to step in to provide service and without an adequate training program for Mike's employees, the service levels were atrocious.

The independent contractor network had to get involved in too many service issues and had to constantly kick an issue up over a service employee's head to a supervisor to get anything resolved. That meant they had to waste time servicing rather than selling. If they could not spend their time selling, they would be out of business soon.

When the employee told Mike the Manager this, Mike the Manager went ballistic. He shouted at the employee that the problem was the employee's fault and that he should resolve the issues. Mike was not going to do the employee's job for him. Mike shot the messenger.

Mike also said to the employee, how dare this individual contractor tell Mike how to run his business? After all, if I can't interfere in his business to get activity reports, then he can't interfere in how I run my business.

Mike told the employee to terminate the top producing independent contractor's contract. Mike did not want him creating more issues for Mike with this independent contractor network. There was never any thought about trying to meet with the independent contractor or to actually think the independent contractor might be right.

CHAPTER 13

Lenny left the call with the independent contractors and headed back to his office to plan his next day. Lenny tried to never leave the office until he was ready for the next day.

That way he could relax at home without worrying about what lay in front of him the next day. It also enabled him to get a quick start on his day when he arrived at the office the following day. There was no scrambling to figure out what he needed to do first. His day was set before he arrived.

Lenny quickly went to his offensive "to do" list. Lenny always kept two "to do" lists...one for the offensive or proactive items he needed to work on and the second was for the defensive items he would need to work on.

Lenny knew that the only way that his organization could achieve their goals was to be proactive and to spend time on the items that allowed an organization to grow. In sports, if you spend all of your time on the defense, you are not likely to score. You have to be on the offensive to score.

He also knew that the tyranny of the urgent could destroy an organization. The tyranny of the urgent is the combination of those items that one needs to take care of in the course of a day like returning phone calls, answering emails, responding to questions, etc. One could spend all of their time doing those urgent items and spend no time on the items that really drive sales and profits. It could relieve a lot of tension to scratch those items off the "to do" list but that would not advance the ball to a point where you could score. He needed his organization working on the high payoff items. They needed to spend more time on offense than defense.

Lenny felt that if he kept just one list the proactive items or the offense could get lost during the course of the day. As a result he kept two lists and encouraged his associates to do the same.

He also prioritized his "to do" lists by designating the items that were the top priority, items that needed to be done but not nearly as critical to have done right away, and finally, items of a lower priority that can be done at any time. He labeled those A for the top items, B for the secondary items, and C for the lowest priority items. Within those three priorities, he labeled those A1 as the item most important in the top category, A2 for the next important item, and continued through all of the items.

Lenny knew that if he planned his day, he was in charge of the day and his work. If he did not, he knew it was easy to get off track and miss key items that needed to be done for the success of his organization.

The organization knew that Lenny subscribed to the theory that a "Lack of planning by someone should not create an emergency for the organization or for another associate." Lenny had been in an organization where things that could have been avoided had someone planned and used their time better became an incredible, last minute, emergency for either him or someone else or, even worse, a lot of people in the organization.

Meanwhile, down the road, Mike the Manager, was on his way out the door. He never planned for the following day. In fact, he didn't even keep one "to do" list, much less one for offense, and one for defense. Mike felt he would remember everything he needed to be done. He thought a to do list was a waste of time.

Mike would come in the next morning and see what needed his attention. He had actually missed meetings in the past because they started earlier than he started the day and had not remembered he had a meeting that early. He did not care. He felt someone should have reminded him of the meeting. It was never his fault.

He was also the boss. If he missed a meeting, the people would just have to adjust to his schedule and review with him when it was more convenient for Mike.

Mike also was the individual in the organization who was always creating emergencies for everyone else for his lack of planning. Since Mike never planned his time, he was always creating an emergency for his organization or someone else.

CHAPTER 14

While Lenny was finishing his day, some of his key associates were meeting without Lenny's knowledge. They had nominated Lenny for Best Leader of the Year and Lenny was one of the finalists for the award.

The organization sponsoring the award had sent one of their representatives to Lenny's organization without Lenny knowing it to interview several employees about what made Lenny such a good leader. The organization wanted to know why the employees felt that Lenny was such a good leader.

One of the associates began by saying that Lenny is real and he is who he says he is. His actions mirror his words and he walks the talk. The associate knew that actions spoke more loudly than words and that you always pay more attention to what someone does than what they say.

Another associate said that Lenny has solid core values. We never have to worry that he may be cheating, lying or stealing. We never have to worry about the company being exposed on a news channel or on the front page of a newspaper. This is a company where the results and the sales growth are real. There is never any worry that someone is "cooking the books".

A third associate indicated that Lenny was an excellent communicator. He always communicates to us his vision of the organization, what we need to do to obtain that vision, how we are doing with attaining that vision, and how we are going to celebrate hitting that target.

She continued by saying that we never have to read between the lines to figure out what is going on in the organization. We never worry about him "spinning" the news. He is candid and honest with us.

The associates continued their session with the interviewer and the interviewer recorded their thoughts:

- He has high expectations of us.
- He will not tolerate less than exceptional performance.
- He "actively" listens to us. When we are meeting with him, he puts down his pen, he doesn't look at his BlackBerry to see what emails or messages he has coming in, and he doesn't allow interruptions. When we are with him, we feel we have 100% of his attention.
- We all know that he is the boss, but we never feel that he holds

that over our heads like a threat. We know he is the boss and we respect him. Respect is not an entitlement; he earns our respect every day.

- He knows that there are no shortcuts and that it is what you do everyday that counts.
- He cares about this company and about every one of us. He respects us.
- He recognizes us for our performance and when he feels there is room for improvement, he lets us know. If the room for improvement is with a person, he has that discussion with the person in private and never in front of anyone else.
- His enthusiasm and his energy are contagious!
- Lenny wants our input. We feel we are a part of the organization and not just along for the ride. We are a part of the decision making process.

- Lenny provides an environment that is rich in diversity. He makes sure that we don't use a "cookie cutter" approach to hiring people where everyone looks and thinks the same way. He wants different perspectives to make sure that we are successful.
- Everyone feels safe and there is no worry that your feedback or your opinion will get you terminated.
- His ego does not get in his or our way as the boss' ego in so many organizations does.
- He is extremely confident and we feel confident in his abilities but his confidence can never be construed as arrogance.
- He insists that we keep growing as people.
- He does not confuse or let us confuse our "Oughtabe's with our Realities". While the economy ought to be better or something else "oughtabe" working better, the Realities are what we have to

deal with. We don't spend time whining about what should be going on. We deal with the reality.

- We also know that for all of us and Lenny especially, our differential advantage we offer this company is our ability to get the job done no matter obstacles we face. We know Lenny is always finding a way to keep this organization moving forward and as a result, we do the same thing.
- Lenny knows that Leadership is not a Spectator Sport. He is visible to us and to our customers and prospects and shows up to play everyday.
- Lenny makes us want to be better.

The interviewer was incredibly impressed with what he had heard and combined with the financial results of this company he was going to recommend Lenny for the award. He also thought about applying to work with this organization himself.

Meanwhile, Mike the Manager's employees never entertained a thought about recommending Mike for Leader of the Year. They thought about nominating him for Worst Leader of the Year, but did not want to waste the time it would take to nominate him for that. They knew that award would not make him want to be any better. They also knew they would not work with him long. They decided that enough was enough and they were leaving Mike.

One Day With Two Leaders

ABOUT THE AUTHOR

D. Lane Stephens, CLU has been in the Insurance Business for 35 years, managing and leading sales organizations for over 30 years. His leadership practices and theories go beyond the insurance business and would apply to anyone in a leadership role. Lane and his wife Michele live in Paradise Valley, Arizona. They have three children, one daughter-in-law and one granddaughter.